Thank you for every moment in life - for they have given me so much wisdom and strength - and continue to do so.

Copyright © Shirley Harvey 2017
All rights reserved. No part of this book may be reproduced, transmitted, or stored in an information retrieval system in any form or by any means, graphic, electronic, or mechanical, including photocopying, taping, and recording, without prior written permission from the publisher.

First edition 2017
ISBN 978-1-7750646-4-0

Published by Animal Publications in a magical place called Shirley World.
www.shirleyharvey.com

let it go

Written and Illustrated by Shirley Harvey

I set an intention

Of a world that I wanted

And a life that I dreamed of,

But then I was daunted.

I didn't yet know

How to make it all happen.

It all felt so big

That I started to sadden.

Every step that I took

Seemed costly or wrong,

But I just kept on going,

Bumbling along.

I was lead down long paths,

Unexpected and fun,

And I ended up where

My intention began.

There's here and now,
There's there and then,
And so much doubt
About if and when.

But we can't do anything
About what's in the past
Or what's in the future
Or what happened last.

We only have
The here and now,
And a chance to enjoy it
And make it WOW!

A fluffy dog

And a hairy hog

Were sitting in the rain.

The fluffy dog

Said to the hairy hog,

"Isn't this rain a pain!

"It's getting me wet

and ill, I bet!"

moaned the soggy dog.

"But it's getting me wet

and the mud's the best yet!"

said a very happy hog.

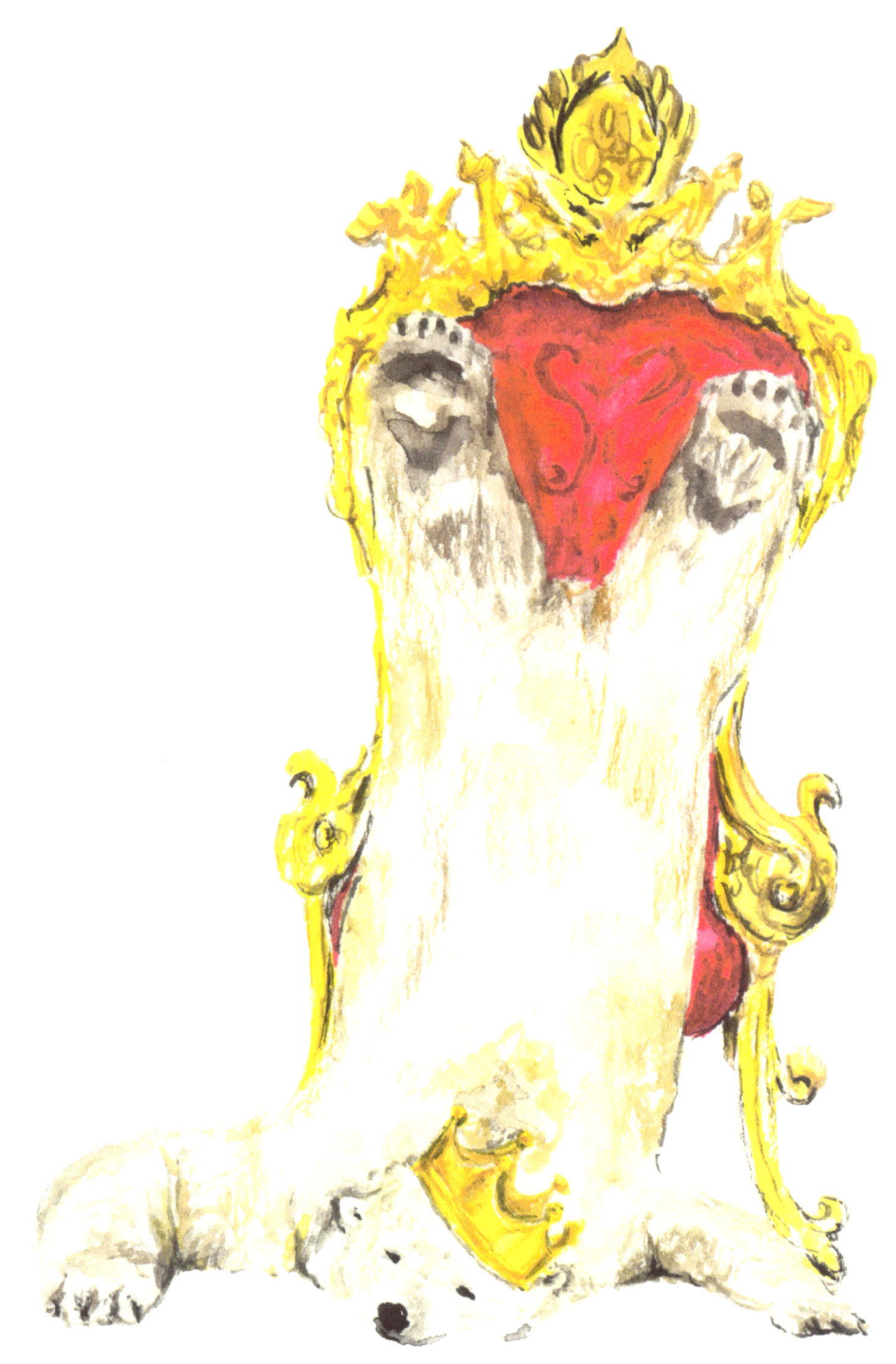

The king sat aloft,

Haughty and proud

And said to his fold,

Boastful and loud,

"I am the King,

The best in this place.

You will not find

A more handsome face."

And with that he stood,

Forgetting the height of his chair,

And fell on his face,

What a dear, silly bear!

I saw his face light up the night,

And I wanted to kiss him with all my might.

I blew him kisses but they missed his face

And travelled far out into outer space.

There they multiplied a thousand fold

And granted the wishes of young and old,

And they granted my wish to plant a kiss

On his face, that wouldn't miss.

So I climbed up high to declare my love

And found something greater up above,

That when I reached for the moon and Mars

I got to play amongst the stars.

You never did see
A more odd little pair
Than the octopus
And the little brown bear.

They saw their differences
And they saw their sames.
It gave them more fun
When playing their games.

The cow jumped over the moon,

Not caring she looked like a loon,

For she knew the secret to happiness is

You can never let go too soon.

letting go

Be a leader, a maker, a trailblazer,
Be a mover and a shaker too.
Be authentically you and never a faker,
And you'll lead with a purpose that's true.

Nigglesome Nigel had many a trouble,

A big one, a small one and one in a bubble.

He'd hide them but find them again and again,

Despite his best efforts, they'd always remain,

He never did meet them, squarely face on,

So he never did solve them, not even one.

"I want, I want, I want it all!"
said the one who was very tall.
"I'll reach up higher than everyone
and eat all the best fruit nearest the sun."

And so she began to eat each single one,
Pausing to look smugly up at the sun,
Who shone down on her from high up above
And warmed her heart with his infinite love.

For the sun always shone, and never did ask
For anything back, for doing this task.
The tall one saw his endless light,
Then stopped and decided to do what was right.

sharing

Looking for a sign of what he should do,

This little shrew, he hadn't a clue.

He couldn't decide to go forwards or back,

So he lost his balance and fell with a whack.

"Why do you fight me?

Does it bring you peace?

Does it make you feel good

When you lunge at my fleece?

Does it make you feel powerful and strong

When you encourage me to believe that I'm always wrong?"

"I guess," said Lion, "It does sometimes."

"Sometimes I wish you'd be more like me,

Stick up for yourself, be mighty, see?

Sometimes I feel like you inside,

Small, weak, wanting to hide.

So that's when I shout and get angry at you.

I hurt you because I see me in you."

There once was a zebra called Debra

Who always stood out from the crowd.

The others would say

She'd look better our way,

But Debra stayed colourful and proud.

Make friends with your fears and you will go far,

Invite them along, let them jump in your car.

They'll come along anyway, like it or not,

Shouting directions and grumbling a lot.

Let them feel welcome but advise them so,

That you are the one who'll decide where to go.

Be, in all your wonderful being-ness
x

Shirley is an artist, writer, entrepreneur and mother with a sweet and whimsical take on the world.

Using her unique style of painting and writing, and her team of trusted animal friends, she brings to light the finer qualities and quirks of what it means to be human with humour and grace.

www.shirleyharvey.com

www.ingramcontent.com/pod-product-compliance
Lightning Source LLC
LaVergne TN
LVHW071032070426
835507LV00003B/128